MORE BUSES WORTH SPOTTING

Mel Kirtley

Preface

My previous book **WHEN BUSES WERE WORTH SPOTTING** concentrated upon the activities of fifteen major north east operators during the fifties and sixties.

In this, the sequel to that title, **MORE BUSES WORTH SPOTTING** recalls some of the smaller independents from that era which were not included in the previous book, as well as unearthing some previously unpublished photographs of buses from the larger undertakings.

As the theme of the book is buses on the roads of North East England, it has enabled me to justify the inclusion of photographs of some vehicles which were visiting the area. It has been a pleasure to recall some of the gems from the likes of *EAST YORKSHIRE, YORKSHIRE TRACTION, RIBBLE* and *POTTERIES* fleets, whether they were working a Limited Stop, Day Trip or Football Special.

I am sure you will agree that every photograph in this book is of a bus worth spotting.

Mel Kirtley
1995

Acknowledgements

I would like to thank the following people, without whose support and assistance the publication of this book would have been greatly delayed.

Principally, my thanks are extended to the Management and Staff of Northeast Press, publishers of The Sunderland Echo. In particular, I must thank Stuart Bell (Managing Director) both for his support and for the loan of the colour transparencies to use on the book cover. Alex Bayley-Kaye has once again been extremely supportive and without her assistance I would still be tying together the numerous loose ends of the book. I must also thank Chris Jones for his artistic guidance with respect to the book cover. Also, a big thank you to Gilbert Johnston and his staff for preparing the photographic material.

Finally, my appreciation to Stuart Bell, Bill Day and Allan Purvis for helping to identify some of the more obscure vehicles whose photographs are included here.

OPERATORS INCLUDED:

Sunderland Corporation
Newcastle Corporation
South Shields Corporation
Darlington Corporation
Stockton Corporation
Hartlepool Corporation
West Hartlepool Corporation
Middlesbrough Corporation

Northern General
Sunderland District
Gateshead & District
Tynemouth & District
Wakefields Motors
Tyneside Tramsways & Tramroads

United
Durham District

Economic
Venture
W H Jolly
OK Motors
TMS
Gillett Brothers
Charlton
Hall Brothers
Carney
Hylton Castle
General
Bee Line
Armstrong
Wilkinson

Yorkshire Woollen
Yorkshire Traction
West Yorkshire
East Yorkshire
Samuel Ledgard
Ribble
Scout
North Western
Lancashire United
Crosville
Potteries
Trent
Scottish Omnibuses

*During the mid-fifties, **SUNDERLAND CORPORATION** carried out a large scale modernisation programme at Fulwell Depot. This included the installation of a new Dawson portable bus washing machine. No. 176, a Crossley bodied Guy Arab IV, is seen here benefiting from a wash and brush up.*
(Photograph courtesy of Sunderland Echo)

*En route to Edinburgh in 1953, this AEC Regal was delivered to **UNITED** in 1937 but did not enter service until the following year. Originally numbered AR014 with Brush body, it was re-bodied by Willowbrook in 1950 at which point it became AR13. When withdrawn in 1955, the chassis of AR13 was cut up and the body used on BG201, the original body of this latter bus having been seriously damaged in an accident.*
(Mel Kirtley collection)

*The first company to transfer its services to the then newly formed **DURHAM DISTRICT SERVICES** in 1950 was Darlington Triumph. This latter company had itself just been formed in December 1949 by the re-naming of the Underwood Bus Company. With the business came this Northern Counties lowbridge bodied Guy Arab 1 dating from 1943 and seen here at Darlington in 1957.*
(Mel Kirtley collection)

*One of many similar coaches operating in the **RIBBLE** fleet during the sixties, No. 812 was an all Leyland combination. It is seen resting at Manors Park, Newcastle, in 1963.*

***SAMUEL LEDGARD** was a West Yorkshire based operator whose fleet contained a fascinating mix of second hand vehicles. KUP 949 was a Leyland/Duple combination that had been new to Iveson of Esh during the fifties. It is seen here "back home" in the north east at Newcastle in 1963. This Leyland Tiger PS1 is now preserved.*

NEWCASTLE CORPORATION'S Nos. 283 and 258 line up at Haymarket during 1963. The former was an all Leyland PD2/1 from 1950 while the latter, from the previous year, was a NCB bodied AEC Regent 111.

*As an inevitable consequence of BTC control, the vast majority of new deliveries to **WEST YORKSHIRE ROAD CAR COMPANY** during the fifties and sixties were standardised upon Bristol chassis and ECW bodywork. This early fifties coach, EBW10, was no exception. It is seen here resting at Newcastle's Haymarket bus station in 1963.*

7

*BUT17 is seen here at Wellington Street bus station, Leeds in 1963. It was one of a trio of Bristol LS6Bs delivered in 1955, principally for use on **UNITED'S** Tyne-Tees-Thames service.*

*KWY 951, a Duple bodied Bedford SB, first entered service with British Ropes of Doncaster in 1952. It was sold to W. H. Jolly of South Hylton in 1960 in whose ownership it operated for one year before being sold to **GENERAL OMNIBUS COMPANY** in Chester-le-Street. It is seen here at General's depot in 1963.*

*This 1963 scene in West Hartlepool captures No. 70 in the **WEST HARTLEPOOL CORPORATION** fleet on an autumn day. No. 70 was a Leyland PD2/3 with Leyland 56 seat bodywork dating from 1950.*

*This bus was new to Yorkshire Woollen in 1936 as their No. 370. It was delivered to the West Yorkshire company as a Leyland TS7 with Roe B32F bodywork and together with twenty four of its brethren it was loaned to **NORTHERN GENERAL** in 1948. The following year all the loan vehicles were transferred to Northern at which point this bus was numbered 1319 in the north east fleet and was partially re-bodied by Picktree Coachbuilders. It was withdrawn by Northern in 1955 and sold to Durham County Council.*
(Mel Kirtley collection)

The Daimler Fleetline revolutionised double deck bus operation in Sunderland during the early sixties. No. 250, seen here at the works of Charles H Roe of Leeds, arrived in Sunderland in April 1962. It was the first of thirty-nine Fleetlines delivered to **SUNDERLAND CORPORATION** *between 1962 and 1966.*

(Mel Kirtley collection)

This lower deck photograph of the first Daimler Fleetline to enter service with **SUNDERLAND COPORATION** *shows the latest state of the art interior bus design of the early sixties.*
(Mel Kirtley collection)

*This photograph shows former **NORTHERN GENERAL** No. 603, a Short bodied AEC Regal from 1934, following its withdrawal from passenger service in 1955 and subsequent sale to a dealer in London.*
(Mel Kirtley collection)

*LLE4 spent some fifteen years in the **UNITED** fleet, from 1937 to 1952. This Leyland TS7 had Brush C30R bodywork and for the last two years of its working life with United, it was demoted from coaching duties to express work on the Limited Stop service.*
(Mel Kirtley collection)

CARNEY was a Sunderland based operator with a small but varied fleet of vehicles. JWF 791 was an unusual Leyland/Beccols combination seen here in Sunderland during 1963.

*BRC 319 began life with Trent before being sold to **BEE LINE ROADWAYS** at whose depot it was photographed during 1963. A Burlingham bodied AEC.*

One of a pair of Roe bodied Crossleys which were new to **SOUTH SHIELDS CORPORATION** *in 1948. No. 144 at Market Square in 1963.*

HVO 913 in the colours of **TRIMDON MOTOR SERVICES** *when photographed at Roker Promenade, Sunderland in 1963, having carried Sunderland football supporters from County Durham for a home game. An interesting AEC/Willowbrook combination.*

SUNDERLAND DIST-RICT'S No. 243 came from a batch of ten buses which were the first underfloor engined vehicles to be purchased by the Northern General group. Dating from 1951, they were Leyland PSU1/9s with Brush bodywork and were the first in the fleet to carry the larger destination display and route numbers, from new. Another interesting feature of the batch was that they had just a single seat at the nearside front, which was intended to improve passenger flow. No. 243 off duty at Park Lane, Sunderland, in 1962.

GATESHEAD & DISTRICT was the first of the Northern General group of companies to take delivery of the Leyland Atlantean. The first ten Atlanteans took to the road in 1959 and were Alexander bodied versions, of which No. 86 was an example.

*DBL13, a front entrance Bristol Lodekka in the **DURHAM DISTRICT** fleet, prepares for a journey to Wingate in 1962. It is pictured here at Park Lane in Sunderland with an "off duty" Leyland PD3 from the Sunderland District fleet standing behind.*

*VNL 44 in the **ARMSTRONG** fleet was a Bedford SB with Duple body. It is seen here at Park Lane, Sunderland in 1963. A LS5G stands immediately behind.*

*Nos. 4 and 72 in the **NEWCASTLE CORPORATION** fleet await disposal at Byker Depot during 1963. No. 4, a Daimler CWA6, was new in 1946 when it was fitted with a second hand Park Royal body from former bus No. 144 which had been new in 1931. No. 4 acquired a new Mann Egerton body in 1950 which it retained until its withdrawal and sale to Dunston Autospares in 1963. Meanwhile, No. 72 was a MCCW bodied Daimler CVG6 from 1948 and was one of fourteen buses in the Newcastle fleet to be delivered with Birmingham styled bodies comprising straight staircases and single line indicators. These were later altered to Newcastle design, the buses having been accepted in 1948 as a means of securing early delivery. No. 72 was withdrawn from service in 1961 and stood at Byker Depot until its eventual sale to Dunston Autospares in 1963.*

__MIDDLESBROUGH CORPORATION__ No. 63 was one of sixteen Leyland PD1/3s delivered in 1949 with ECW bodies. They were the first 8ft. wide buses delivered to Middlesbrough. No. 63 was withdrawn in 1962.
(Photograph courtesy of Photobus/G. Turner)

*Ex **UNITED** bus GGL4 is seen here with Greyhound of Sheffield following its sale by United in 1955. This bus was new in 1944 as a Northern Counties bodied Guy Arab 11 which was built to wartime specifications.*
(Mel Kirtley collection)

*BTJ 63, an ex **LANCASHIRE UNITED** vehicle, was being used as a mobile home when seen here on some waste ground at East Boldon, near Sunderland.*

*Pictured "off duty" at **DARLINGTON CORPORATION'S** depot is No. 57, a Roe H61R bodied Guy Arab 1V which was delivered to the undertaking in 1956.*
(Photograph courtesy of Photobus/G. Turner)

*One of six AEC Regals with 30 seat Duple coach bodies delivered to **NORTHERN GENERAL** in January 1939. No. 931 is seen here on a day trip to the Lake District during the early fifties.*
(Mel Kirtley collection)

HYLTON CASTLE MOTORS was a Sunderland based operator which, in the sixties, boasted a varied collection of new and second hand vehicles. KOD 590 fell very much into the second category and it started life with Devon General. It is seen here at Hylton Castle's Southwick Depot in 1964. The Weymann bodywork on this AEC typifies British bus design of the forties.

This Picktree bodied Guy Arab LUF was one of twelve delivered to Northern General during 1954. Eight of the batch were sold to SAMUEL LEDGARD of West Yorkshire during the early sixties. Former Northern General No. 1538 made a return visit to its native Tyneside on a day trip in 1963 in the colours of Ledgard.

*Bus No. 36 in the **SUNDERLAND CORPORATION** fleet was one of twelve 'Piano Front' Roe bodied Daimlers which were delivered to the undertaking during 1934-1936. It is seen here at Fulwell Depot suitably decorated for the Queen's Coronation. It was later used as a snowplough and it was one of the longest survivors in the Sunderland fleet when it was finally disposed of in 1960.*
(Photograph courtesy of Sunderland Echo)

*This Roe H48C bodied Leyland Titan TD7 was new to **WEST HARTLEPOOL CORPORATION TRANSPORT** in 1942. It is now preserved and is seen here at a rally in Seaburn, Sunderland.*

*In pristine condition, **SUNDERLAND DISTRICT** No. 320 stands at the company's Philadelphia depot. It was one of a pair of Leyland PSUC1/2s with Burlingham C41F bodywork, new in 1961. It remained in SDO's coach fleet until its withdrawal in 1974, eventually becoming a mobile home in Southport in 1975.*

***EAST YORKSHIRE MOTOR SERVICES** No. 681 was one of eight Leyland Tiger Cub PSUC1/2s with Metro Cammell DP41F bodywork built for the company in 1960. It looks immaculate as it poses for the camera at Manors Park, Newcastle, in 1963. Standing alongside is a Northern General Saro bodied Leyland PSUC1/1.*

UNITED'S GGL1 was a Guy Arab 11 with Brush L27/28R bodywork built to wartime specifications during 1944. ·It was originally numbered GDO1. It was photographed in Middlesbrough in 1955 shortly before withdrawal.
(Mel Kirtley collection)

This exotic looking scene — at Ripon — captures BG30 and BG442 on camera in 1955. BG30 was a Bristol L5G with ECW body and was from a batch of twenty delivered in 1938 which were the first Bristol L chassis built for UNITED. This bus was sold to a dealer in 1957. Meanwhile, BG442 was an ECW bodied Bristol L5G, new in 1950 and built to standard BTC specifications.
(Mel Kirtley collection)

GUP 569 was acquired by **DURHAM DISTRICT SERVICES** *together with the business of ABC Motor Services, Ferryhill on 31st December 1950. This 1946 Dennis Lancet J3 had its original Raine body replaced in 1956 by Willowbrook bodywork removed from United's AR12, an AEC Regal.*
(Mel Kirtley collection)

The post-war fleet intakes of South Shields and nearby Sunderland followed largely parallel paths. Both operators purchased significant numbers of Guy and Daimler vehicles and these were invariably bodied by Charles H. Roe of Leeds. No. 149 in the **SOUTH SHIELDS CORPORATION** *fleet rests at Market Square during a summer day in 1963.*

*Standing at the Bishop Auckland depot of **OK MOTORS** in 1963, this Plaxton bodied AEC Reliance was new in 1957 and gave seventeen years service to the company.*

AECs and Leylands with Weymann Fanfare bodywork were to be found in most BET fleets during the fifties and sixties.
***NORTH WESTERN** No. 570 was an AEC Reliance with overdrive gearbox and was an exhibit at the 1954 Commercial Motor Show. This photograph was taken at Haymarket bus station, Newcastle, in 1963.*

*This Massey bodied AEC Regent 111 was from a batch of twenty which were new to **NEWCASTLE CORPORATION** in 1949. It is seen here at Byker Depot awaiting its fate in 1963. It had been withdrawn from passenger service during the previous year.*

*By the time this photograph was taken in May 1963, **WEST YORKSHIRE ROAD CAR COMPANY'S** SGL11 was thirteen years old and had just completed one of its last express services into Newcastle.*

*GCU 571 in the **HALL BROTHERS** fleet journeys along Stockton Road, Sunderland in 1963. The Duple bodywork on this Leyland coach was typical of early sixties manufacture.*

***CHARLTON'S** ONL 986, a Bedford/Duple combination poses for the camera at Haymarket bus station, Newcastle while a United L5G stands alongside.*

*DARLINGTON CORPORATION'S No. 80 seen here during the early sixties had a distinct utility appearance about it. It was built in 1950 and comprised Guy Arab chassis and Roberts bodywork.
(Photograph courtesy of Photobus/G. Turner)*

GUA 782 first entered service with Leeds City Transport in 1938 as a Roe bodied Leyland TD5. It was purchased by **OK MOTORS** *in 1950 and became a tree lopper for the company in January 1960. It was sold for scrap in 1967.*

The early sixties witnessed the transfer of a large number of buses from the fleets of **NORTHERN GENERAL'S** associated companies to that of the parent company. Gatehead & District, Sunderland District and Tynemouth & District all lost buses to the Northern fleet at that time. This included former Gateshead & District vehicles Nos. 17 and 31 which were re-numbered 1939 and 2040 by Northern when acquired in 1960 and 1962 respectively. BCN 617 (above) was one of twenty Guy Arab 111 5LWs with Guy bodies on Park Royal frames, delivered to Gateshead in 1950. BCN 872 (below) was a Brush bodied Guy Arab 111 5LW and was from a batch of nine which were new to Gateshead in 1950.

SOUTH SHIELDS CORPORATION *continued to purchase rear platform Daimlers well into the mid sixties at a time when the Fleetline and Atlantean was the chosen bus of most municipal operators. No. 129 was a Daimler CSG6 with a smart Roe 65 seat body.*

BJ61 was a EC0C bodied Bristol J05G, new to **UNITED** *in 1936. It was one of a batch of sixty four buses which were delivered to United at that time and when finally withdrawn in 1956, it was one of the last survivors from the batch. It subsequently gave further PSV service with LMT of Salford. It is seen here at Scarborough in 1952.*
(Mel Kirtley collection)

*NEH 408 started life with **POTTERIES MOTOR TRACTION** as their No. SN415 when this Lawton bodied AEC Regal became the first half cab single decker delivered to that operator. By the time this photograph was taken the vehicle had joined the fleet of **TRIMDON MOTOR SERVICES** and made regular fortnightly trips to Roker Park during the football season. It is seen here in Sunderland during 1963.*

*This Burlingham bodied Leyland Tiger Cub was operated by **WILKINSON** of Sedfield during the fifties and sixties. TPT 448 at Bishop Auckland in 1963.*

In 1946, **SUNDERLAND CORPORATION** took delivery of three Crossleys fitted with square fronted, all metal boldies by Craven. The appearance of these buses reflected immediate post-war austerity and they were the first Sunderland buses to be fitted with a rear 'Stop' light. Upon the arrival of Norman Morton as Transport Manager in 1952, the undertaking embarked upon a fuel economy drive, at which point these buses had their Crossley engines replaced by Gardner 5LW engines. No. 20 is seen out of town at Chester-le-Street on private hire work.
(Photograph courtesy of Photobus)

MPT 470 is seen here in December 1963, awaiting disposal by **OK MOTORS** to whom it was new in 1951 as a AEC Regal/Willowbrook re-build. The vehicle was acquired as chassis only from the London Passenger Transport board where it had been numbered T60 (GF 527). In its former life, this AEC Regal had been fitted with a LGOC body. MPT 470 was sold for scrap in 1964.

One of seventy four trolleybuses ordered by **NEWCASTLE CORPORATION** to serve a joint operation with the Gateshead & District Tramways Company. Plans for the joint service were aborted when the Gateshead company's sudden change of policy resulted in their trams being replaced by motor buses rather than by trolleybuses. Thus, Newcastle Corporation were left with a surplus of vehicles and, as a consequence, many of their pre-war trolleybuses were prematurely withdrawn from passenger service. Of the seventy four deliveries from 1950, twenty four were Sunbeam F4s with NCB bodies and fifty were BUT 9641Ts with MCCW bodies. No. 622 was an example of the latter combination and is seen here at Byker in 1963. It survived with Newcastle until the abandonment of the trolleybus system in 1966.

No. 112 in the **MIDDLESBROUGH CORPORATION** fleet is seen here in service shortly after delivery in 1962. This Daimler Fleetline was bodied by Northern Counties and was eventually transferred to the fleet of Teesside Municipal Transport in 1968.
(Photograph courtesy of Photobus/G. Turner)

*This winter scene catches former **UNITED** vehicle LGL14 looking rather forlorn as it stands at York following its sale to D. E. & L. A. Hope (Contractors). It had been new to United in 1930 as a Leyland L24/24R bodied Leyland TD1. It was withdrawn in December 1950 and served as a contractor's vehicle for seven years before eventually becoming a holiday caravan at Crimdon Dene.*
(Mel Kirtley collection)

*VF 2741 first entered service with **UNITED** in 1928 with standard 35 seat bus bodywork. It later became one of ten similar vehicles to be fitted with new Plaxton bodies. The re-bodied vehicles were suitably equipped for operation on Scarborough's sea front service.*
(Mel Kirtley collection)

*In 1929, **YORKSHIRE WOOLLEN DISTRICT TRANSPORT COMPANY** became a member of the Limited Stop 'pool' of companies which operated a long distance service between Newcastle and Manchester via Leeds. North east companies in the 'pool' were Northern General and United. No. 887 was one of fifteen AEC Reliances with Marshall B43F bodywork delivered to Yorkshire Woollen in 1962. It is seen here working the Limited Stop X97 service at Worswick Street, Newcastle in 1963.*

*No. 1053 in the **RIBBLE** fleet was caught by the camera in 1963 on Limited Stop duties at Worswick Street, Newcastle, and was being closely pursued by a Northern General Atlantean.*

One of seven Leyland PD2/40s with Roe bodywork delivered to **WEST HARTLEPOOL CORPORATION** *in 1961 which were similar to an earlier batch which entered service with this operator some three years previously. No. 8 at Old Hartlepool Road in 1963.*

A relatively small number of Bristol LS5Gs were fitted with Cave-Brown-Cave heating systems. This example from 1958 was numbered SUG64 in the **WEST YORKSHIRE ROAD CAR COMPANY** *fleet and was photographed at Haymarket, Newcastle in 1963.*

*Marlborough Crescent bus station in Newcastle was heavily populated by the yellow and maroon buses of the **VENTURE TRANSPORT COMPANY** throughout the fifties and sixties. Bus 175, a Willowbrook bodied Atkinson Alpha, stirs fond memories as it awaits passengers in the afternoon sunshine during 1962.*

*DBL3 was one of the first buses purchased new by **DURHAM DISTRICT SERVICES**. It joined the fleet in 1956 as an ECW bodied Bristol LD6B. It is seen here at Leadyard, Darlington, with a L5G standing immediately behind.*

*No. 175 was one of ten AEC Regent Vs delivered to **NEWCASTLE CORPORATION** in 1957. A further ten lowbridge versions of the bus were also delivered during the same year for the Ponteland route. All twenty buses had bodywork by Park Royal. No. 175 remained in service long enough to be transferred to the fleet of Tyneside PTE which assumed control of Newcastle's activities in 1970.*

*JXN 356, a Leyland 7RT with 56 seat Park Royal body was one of eight RTs acquired from London Transport in March 1958. It had been new to London Transport in 1949 and was finally sold by **OK MOTORS** in 1970 after giving twelve years service to the Bishop Auckland based operator. Standing alongside is a United MW5G.*

*Former **TRIMDON MOTOR SERVICES** OUP 579 was photographed in Dewsbury shortly after its sale to Longstaff of Mirfield in Yorkshire.*

*Leyland LPT 489 was built at the coachworks of ACB in Southwick, Sunderland during the late forties. It is seen here just yards from its place of manufacture in 1964 in the colours of **HYLTON CASTLE MOTORS**.*

Another bus to be acquired by **NORTHERN GENERAL** *from one of its associated companies, this time Tynemouth & District, was FT 9916 which had been numbered 216 by Tynemouth, when new in 1957. It was re-numbered 2261 by Northern when absorbed into their fleet in 1962 where it served until 1971. It is pictured here at Marlborough Crescent in Newcastle during 1962, soon after transfer.*

Similar to a batch of Northern General buses from the early fifties, **TYNEMOUTH & DISTRICT'S** *No. 186 was from a batch of ten Weymann bodied Guy Arab 111 5LWs which were new to the company in 1952. It is seen here at Percy Main, North Shields, in 1962.*

*One of four trolleybuses in the **SOUTH SHIELDS CORPORATION** fleet to be purchased from Pontypridd Urban District Council in 1957. New in 1945, these Karrier W4s had Park Royal bodies built to fully relaxed specifications. No. 239 remained in service with South Shields until 1964.*

***GILLETT BROTHERS** of Quarrington Hill operated this Burlingham bodied AEC Regal as their No. 20 during the sixties. The coach was one of many parked near Roker Promenade in January 1963, having carried crowds of Sunderland AFC supporters to watch "the lads" playing at home.*

*Two **CROSVILLE** coaches with the inevitable pairing of Bristol chassis and ECW bodywork, CM360 (above) and CMG477 (below) are pictured here at Roker, Sunderland in 1964 awaiting the football crowds.*

During the course of the second world war, twenty three double deck buses were added to the fleet of **SUNDERLAND CORPORATION.** Bodywork was supplied by a variety of companies including Roe, Massey, Pickering and Duple. No. 68, a Pickering bodied Guy Arab 11 5LW, was one of a pair of Pickering utilities and is seen (above) crossing Wearmouth Bridge during the early fifties. Soon after this photograph was taken, No. 68 lost its roof and it subsequently served as an illuminated bus. It was later used as a Promendade Tour bus and operated on the coastal journey between Roker and Whitburn during the summer months. It is pictured (below) being inspected by the Transport Committee following its modification for Promenade Tour duties.
(Mel Kirtley collecton)

*Service 57, a joint operation with Northern General, was one of only two **UNITED** services to operate out of Sunderland's Park Lane bus station in 1962, the year in which this photograph was taken. BBL24 was a 1948 Bristol K6B with the inevitable ECW bodywork.*

*This Bedford C422 was purchased new by **W. H. JOLLY** of South Hylton in 1960 and was operated by that owner for four years before being sold. It was fitted with 29 seat Duple Super Vista bodywork and is seen here at Alnwick in 1961 while working on a Seahouses day trip.*

HARTLEPOOL CORPORATION was a miniature amongst municipal operators which commenced working in August 1953 following the acquisition of four second hand Bristols from London Transport. The undertaking operated just one route, between Hartlepool and West Hartlepool, as a joint service with West Hartlepool Corporation. This was one of four Roe bodied AEC Regent Vs dating from 1956 which was operated on behalf of Hartlepool Corporation by Bee Line Roadways.

*NTJ 248 is seen here in 1963 at the Bishop Auckland depot of **OK MOTORS** as a Duple bodied AEC Regal 111. The vehicle had been new to Florence Motors, Morecambe in 1952 with Plaxton bodywork and was subsequently sold the following year to Wallace Arnold. It was severely damaged in an accident in 1956, at which point a new Duple body — from MUA 497 — was fitted. NTJ 248 made its way to OK Motors via a network of dealers and was withdrawn and sold by OK in 1966.*

*DLC95 sporting the cream and maroon coach livery of **DURHAM DISTRICT SERVICES.** This Gurney Nutting bodied Leyland PS1/1 was acquired with the business of the Express Omnibus Company of Durham in 1950 and is seen here at The Green in Sunderland during 1961. In the background are the premises of one of the town's most popular nightspots of the time — Wetherells Club. DBE21, a 1960 Bristol MW5G with ECW DP41F body stands alongside.*

*DB213 in the **DURHAM DISTRICT** fleet, a Bristol L5G with ECW bodywork stands at Sunderland's Park Lane bus station in 1962 prior to leaving for Darlington. It was one of thirty nine L5Gs transferred from the United fleet to Durham District at that time.*

45

SHOP AT

BINNS

SCT   AMBLESIDE TERRACE

BUS STOP

92

GR 9924

*One of a dozen Daimler CVG6s new to **SUNDERLAND CORPORATION** in 1948 and the first six cylinder Gardner/Daimler combinations to be delivered to this operator. These buses had 56 seat Massey bodies, later re-seated to 58. No. 92 and its crew pose for the camera, prior to leaving for Ambleside Terrace in 1951 when the standard fleet livery was red and cream. The entire batch was extensively re-built by SCT during 1960/1961. No. 92 was one of the last three of the batch to be withdrawn from passenger service when it was sold to Bingley Autospares in 1964.*
(Photograph courtesy of Sunderland Echo)

*No. 2608 spent little more than four years in the **NORTHERN GENERAL** fleet from being new in 1963 to its eventual sale to Heather Bell Motor Services, Tow Law, in 1967. It was one of eight Bedford SB5s with Harrington C41F bodywork. When photographed leaving Marlborough Crescent, Newcastle, in 1963 it was all set for a day in Blackpool.*

*In 1964 when Sunderland AFC were challenging for promotion to Division One, 40,000 crowds were guaranteed and coach parking was not one of the easiest occupations. This Leyland/Plaxton coach, No. 1 in the **TRENT** fleet, was squeezed in amongst an assortment of cars and motor cycles on a Saturday afternoon when Sunderland played hosts to Derby County.*

No. 227, a Roe bodied AEC Regent 111 from 1950, in the fleet of **SUNDERLAND DISTRICT** which during the fifties and sixties was predominated by Leylands. When this photograph was taken, No. 227 was to survive only a matter of weeks in the Sunderland District fleet before being transferred to Northern General as their No. 2045. It remained with this latter operator from September 1962 until March 1965 when it was sold for scrap.

WAKEFIELDS MOTORS came under the operational control of Tynemouth & District and was largely involved in coaching activities. Fleet numbers of Wakefields Motors and Tynemouth & District ran concurrently although up to the mid fifties these were prefixed by the letter W or T respectively. Although some fleet histories list No. 234, seen here, as a Tynemouth vehicle it most certainly carried the name of Wakefields Motors when photographed in Northumberland Square, North Shields, during the summer of 1962. A Leyland PD3/4 with MCCW body dating from 1958.

48

*From 1963, another example of a **STOCKTON UPON TEES CORPORATION** Leyland. This Titan PD2/40 had Weymann Orion H64F bodywork and travels down Stockton High Street on a non market day, as witnessed by the park cars on the traders' pitches.*
(Photograph courtesy of Photobus/G. Turner)

*This Leyland TS8 was another vehicle to find its way into the early **DURHAM DISTRICT** fleet following the takeover of Darlington Triumph services in 1950.*
(Mel Kirtley collection)

YORKSHIRE TRACTION'S No. 1032, photographed here at Durham bus station in 1963, was one of eight Willowbrook DP39F bodied Leyland Tiger Cub PSUC1/2s delivered to the company in 1955.

*Photographed in one of the perimeter streets around Roker Park on a match day in 1964 is No. 37 in the **TRENT** fleet. Classic Weymann Fanfare bodywork on this AEC Reliance was typical of mid fifties deliveries to BET companies. It prepares to take home a coach load of Derby County supporters.*

*BBH29 was from a batch of sixteen Bristol KSW6Bs delivered new to **UNITED** in 1953. It is seen parked up at Haymarket, Newcastle, in 1962 prior to loading for a trip to Seaton Sluice.*

*The name **ECONOMIC** was the fusion of the bus business interests of G. R. Anderson and E. W. Wilson who each operated a coastal service between Sunderland and South Shields. No. 6 in the Anderson fleet was a Plaxton bodied AEC Reliance which was photographed at Derwent Street in Sunderland during 1962 as it approached the company's Park Lane terminus.*

SOUTH SHIELDS CORPORATION'S *abandonment of its trolleybus system took place during 1964. No. 205, seen here at the town's Market Square in 1963, had been new to St. Helens Corporation in 1950 and was purchased by South Shields some nine years later. It was a Sunbeam F4 and was one of the country's few trolleybuses to be built by East Lancs (Bridlington) Ltd. The batch of ten to be transferred from St. Helens were the only 8ft. wide trolleybuses to be operated in South Shields.*

*This most interesting vehicle was new to J. J. Baker of Baker & Gillett of Durham. When Mr Baker died in 1958, the company was re-named **GB MOTORS** (Gillett Brothers). GPT 678, a Raine bodied AEC Regal from 1946, is seen here on some waste ground at West Boldon during 1963.*

NORTH WESTERN No. 795, a Leyland/Willowbrook combination to standard BET specifications of the late fifties, rests at Haymarket, Newcastle, during 1963.

Six Leyland Tiger Cub PSUC1/2s with Burlingham Seagull C41F bodies were delivered to **YORKSHIRE TRACTION** *in 1961. No. 1209 from the batch at Newcastle en route to Barnsley during 1963.*

*Of the seventy new motor buses which entered service in **NEWCASTLE CORPORATION'S** colours during 1950, forty were AEC Regent 111s with distinctive NCB bodywork. One of the batch, No. 341, escaped the breaker's torch and currently awaits preservation. No. 325, seen here, was withdrawn from passenger service in 1966 but was later re-licenced for Driver Training duties until 1969. It crosses Byker Bridge in 1963 when evidence of trolleybus operation was still apparent.*

*KHN 417 came to **DURHAM DISTRICT SERVICES** with the acquisition, of the business of Darlington Triumph. It had been new to the latter company in 1947 as an ACB bodied Guy Arab 111 and was subsequently rebodied with the bodywork of a United Bristol L5G.*
(Mel Kirtley collection)

From the early fifties onwards, virtually every double decker delivered to **MIDDLESBROUGH CORPORATION** *was bodied by Northern Counties. No. 85 a Guy Arab IV 6LW from 1955, was no exception. It is seen here passing Middlesbrough Town Hall.*
(Photograph courtesy of Photobus/G. Turner)

This photograph was taken at the West Hartlepool depot of **BEE LINE ROADWAYS** *in early 1963 and shows two Bedford/Duple combinations, NEF 788 and NEF 789.*

HALL BROTHERS were an extremely active coach operator in the region at the time this photograph was taken. VPM 898, an AEC Reliance, was an ex-Harrington demonstrator and is seen here leaving Newcastle's Marlborough Crescent bus station in 1963.

An excellent example of standard Park Royal bodywork of the early sixties was to be found on this AEC Reliance from the SCOTTISH OMNIBUSES fleet. B704 at Haymarket, Newcastle in 1963.

*No. 75 in the **DARLINGTON CORPORATION TRANSPORT** fleet was an East Lancs bodied Guy Arab 111, seen here outside the company's depot. It was one of a batch of three which were delivered to the undertaking in 1950. (Photograph courtesy of Photobus/G. Turner)*

*A relatively deserted Byker Bridge on a mid-week afternoon in 1963 contrasts sharply with the scene today. No. 220 in the **TYNEMOUTH & DISTRICT** fleet heads from Gateshead with a Morris Mini Minor in pursuit. One of five Leyland PD2/12s with Willowbrook bodies dating from 1957, this was to be the only occasion that the Northern General group used this company to build double deck buses.*

*714 PT in the **GENERAL OMNIBUS COMPANY** fleet at Roker, Sunderland in late 1963. This vehicle had been acquired from Favourite and comprised Bedford chassis and Yeats bodywork.*

*New in 1960, 875 FUP was a Bedford SB5 with Plaxton DP44F bodywork. It is seen resting at the **OK MOTORS** depot at Bishop Auckland during 1963. It was sold by the company in 1971.*

*The first Leyland Atlantean to enter service with **NEWCASTLE CORPORATION** did so in February 1960 and was an Alexander bodied version. Two months later, it was followed by a MCCW bodied Atlantean. During the next two years, a further fifty Leyland Atlanteans joined the Newcastle fleet with choice of bodywork being split between Alexander and Weymann. No. 236 was a Weymann bodied vehicle from 1962 and was photographed at Walker during the following year.*

*An AEC Reliance with Willowbrook DP53F bodywork which was typical of BET fleet intakes of the early sixties. **NORTH WESTERN** No. 941 at Newcastle in 1963.*

WEST HARTLEPOOL CORPORATION'S No. 87, seen here at Old Hartlepool Road in 1963, was a Daimler CVG6 with Roe 58 seat bodywork dating from 1953.

*When **NORTHERN GENERAL** acquired the business of J. W. Hurst & Son of Winlaton in August 1951, it also acquired a fleet of reasonably modern buses. Most of the buses were five years old or less and LUP 753, seen here, was a mere six months old when absorbed into Northern General's fleet. It was one of a pair of Dennis Lancet 3s with bodywork by local company ACB.*
(Mel Kirtley collection)

*The quaintly named **TYNE-SIDE TRAMWAYS & TRAMROADS COMPANY** was the smallest of Northern General's associated companies, operating a fleet of twenty or less vehicles at any one time. Here the crew of No. 48 board the bus at Croft street, Newcastle for the journey to North Shields. Note the absence of a route number box. Bus 48, a MCCW bodied Leyland PD3/4, was one of three buses which were new in 1958 and were initially operated by Tynemouth & District, for some months. All three buses were withdrawn in 1971, No. 48 transferring to Northern General as a driver training vehicle.*

*BBC8 was from a batch of ten Bristol L6Bs with ECW FC31F bodies, purchased for use on the Scarborough sea front service in 1950. In 1960, BBC8 was converted to a mobile information bureau by **UNITED** while still retaining its original fleet number.*

*Two coaches from the **SCOUT** fleet which had carried visiting football supporters to Roker Park in 1964. S63 (above) was a Leyland/Harrington combination while S740 (below), another Leyland, had stylish bodywork by Plaxton.*

SUNDERLAND CORPORATION'S No. 202 was one of sixty-five new buses delivered during the tram replacement programme of 1954. It was exhibited at that year's Commercial Motor Show when it became only the second 27ft. long British bus to seat 65 passengers. It posed for the camera at Fulwell Depot prior to entering service.
(Photograph courtesy of Sunderland Echo)

*One of ten Leyland PSU3/1Rs with Willowbrook bodies delivered to **NORTHERN GENERAL** in July 1960. When seen here at Sunderland's Park Lane bus station, this bus was a mere few months old as it prepared to go west to Consett.*

From the days when a store could close for the day with just a pair of wooden gates as the only security measure, **STOCKTON UPON TEES CORPORATION'S** *No. 103 journeys along the Stockton High Street past the former Blacketts department store in 1963. At this time the undertaking's fleet was standardised entirely upon Leylands; this Titan PD2/40 being bodied by Weymann in 1962.*
(Photograph courtesy of Photobus/G. Turner)

Superbly distinctive bodywork by Burlingham was to be found on **RIBBLE** *Leyland No. 993, seen here at South Shields in 1963.*

SCOTTISH OMNIBUSES No. C112A was a Burlingham bodied Bedford OB. It was photographed on a day trip to Roker, Sunderland in 1964.

136 EMO, an AEC Reliance with smart Duple bodywork, in the fleet of GENERAL OMNIBUS COMPANY at Chester-le-Street bus station in 1963.

*Delivered to **NEWCASTLE CORPORATION** as their No. 10 in 1949, this all Leyland PD2/1 was re-numbered 358 in March 1963 and poses for the camera at Haymarket on first day duty following re-painting and re-numbering. Its original fleet number was allocated to one of the twenty five new Leyland Atlanteans which were delivered to Newcastle in June 1963 as Nos. 1-25.*

*DDC113, a Dennis Yeates built in 1946, was one of many varied vehicles to be found in the **DURHAM DISTRICT** fleet during the fifties as the company systematically acquired businesses of road passenger transport operators in the areas of south and central Durham.*
(Mel Kirtley collection)

*During the early to mid-fifties, **NORTHERN GENERAL** and its associated companies were enthusiastic users of Guy buses and coaches. No. 1416 was one of twenty Guy Arab III 5LWs with Park Royal H30/26R bodywork delivered to Northern in 1952. When photographed at Sunderland's Park Lane bus station in 1961, it was preparing for the relatively short journey to the town's Red House estate, having just completed the trip from Pennywell.*

*Regarded by many as the most attractive single decker to arrive on the scene in the fifties. This Saro bodied Leyland PSUC/1 was one of sixteen delivered to **SUNDERLAND DISTRICT** in 1954 and was similar to a batch delivered to Northern General at that time. No. 271 rests at Park Lane bus station in Sunderland on a summers day in 1962.*

*Working the Limited Stop X97 joint operation out of Newcastle, SMG19 in the fleet of the **WEST YORKSHIRE ROAD CAR COMPANY,** poses for the camera in 1963, shortly after delivery.*

*This AEC Reliance with smart Harrington Wayfarer bodywork was one of the more prestigious members of the **HYLTON CASTLE MOTORS** fleet during the sixties. EM 5477 at Southwick Depot in 1964.*

*LP42/LP12/LP34/LP5 were from a batch of Leyland PS1s with Willowbrook bodies which were delivered to **UNITED** in 1947. The bodies on these buses were built to Tilling standards but were of Willowbrook design. They are seen here minus destination boards, following de-licencing in 1959.*
(Mel Kirtley collection)

*It was "clocking off" time at the shipyards when this photograph was taken in Sunderland in the late fifties. It shows four types of buses in service with **SUNDERLAND CORPORATION** at that time. No. 189, a Crossley bodied Guy Arab 1V en route to Humbledon, stands in the foreground while No. 11, an all Crossley vehicle from 1947, heads in the opposite direction to Town. A Roe bodied Guy and a Roe bodied Daimler pursue No. 189 while another all Crossley vehicle also heads for town.*
(Photograph courtesy of Sunderland Echo)

JTG 948, a Weymann bodied AEC, spent most of its working life with Rhondda in South Wales before being sold to **HYLTON CASTLE MOTORS** *in whose livery it is seen here during 1964.*

With connections on Wearside for over 120 years, the Sunderland **Echo** is pleased to be associated with this historical document and to have assisted with Mr Kirtley's production.

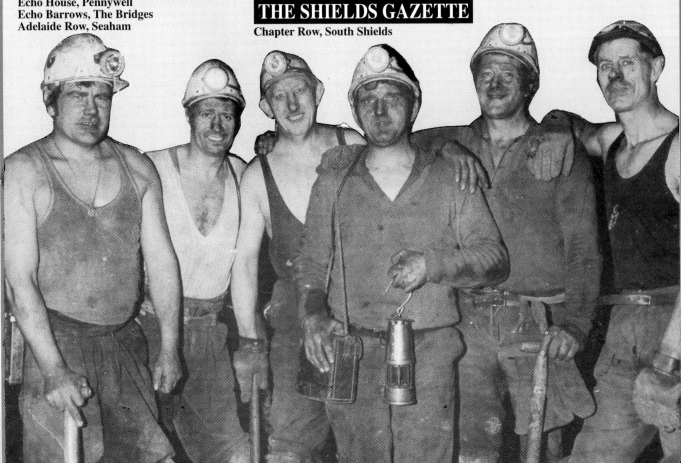